ESP

Stories of Strange Happenings

ESP

Stories of Strange Happenings

by RITA GOLDEN GELMAN

Cover illustration by Stephen Shirak

Inside illustrations by Ted Hanke

SCHOLASTIC BOOK SERVICES

NEW YORK • TORONTO • LONDON • AUCKLAND • SYDNEY • TOKYO

For Mitch and Jan

Editor: Deborah Felder   Designer: Joan Farber

ISBN 0-590-31312-6

12 11 10 9 8 7 6 5 4 3 2 1   1   1 2 3 4 5 6/8

CONTENTS

What is E S P?

The stories in this book are all about ESP — extra-sensory perception.

We hear a lot about ESP these days. What is it? What does "extra-sensory perception" really mean?

We all know about our five senses — sight, touch, taste, smell, and hearing. But, in addition to these, some people seem to have an *extra* sense, through which they can perceive or "see" entire events.

Sometimes a person seems to just "know" what another person is thinking. Sometimes he or she can see what is happening in a distant place. Some people even seem to know about events *before* they happen! It's as though they had received a message from somewhere or someone—an ESP message!

ESP can be about the past, the present, or the future. An ESP message may come as a vague *sense* that something is going to happen. Or it may come in clear, mental pictures with actions, words, and strong feelings.

Most of us have an "extra" sense about things or events now and then. But only a few people seem to receive strong, clear impressions quite often.

The ESP stories in this book were told by real people.* Yet none of the stories contains enough scientific facts to prove that ESP really exists. Scientists have always been baffled by ESP. They can't weigh it, measure it, or X-ray it. All they know is that people have been telling stories of their ESP experiences for thousands of years.

---

*Note: Many of the names used in these stories are fictitious.

Family E S P

Many ESP messages are passed between people who are very close — parents and children, brothers and sisters, or very good friends. And nearly all family ESP stories involve something dramatic—an accident, an illness, a fire, a death. People don't receive ESP messages that a friend or relative is brushing his or her teeth or drinking a glass of milk! ESP messages are usually about very emotional situations.

The following ESP stories have all happened between people who are closely related to each other.

Case #1:

"Mommy! Mommy!"

It was a hot summer day in 1947. The two young Smith children were moping around the house. "Please," they begged their mother. "Please take us to the beach."

But without a car, Mrs. Smith had no way to get to the beach. Then a neighbor came by. She and her children were on their way to the beach. Would the Smith children like to join them?

Mrs. Smith helped her children get ready. They put on their bathing suits, packed their towels, and gathered their beach toys together. Six-year-old Johnny's favorite beach toy was a small rubber boat, just big enough for him to sit in. He loved to paddle himself around in the water. Johnny picked up his boat and climbed into the neighbor's car. Mrs. Smith waved as they drove off.

Several hours later, around three o'clock in the afternoon, Mrs. Smith suddenly felt very uneasy. Her heart began to pound, and her head felt strange. Then, as if there were a TV set inside her head, Mrs. Smith clearly saw a picture of Johnny in his boat. A strong wind was blowing him away from land, out to sea — into deeper and deeper water. Johnny looked terrified. He was unable to steer the boat back to shore.

Mrs. Smith saw the whole scene while she was standing in her house! She could hear Johnny's

voice clearly. "Mommy! Mommy!" he was shouting.

Mrs. Smith was shaking with fear. She wanted to rush to the beach, but she had no way to get there! I've got to call the police, she thought. But what would she tell them? "I have a *hunch* that my son is in trouble"? That was hardly the kind of emergency that would send the police department running!

So Mrs. Smith sat down and closed her eyes. "Stay in the boat, Johnny," she thought, over and over again. "Just stay in the boat until help arrives."

A while later Mr. Smith came home. "I'm going over to the beach for a swim," he announced as he walked in the door. Mrs. Smith said nothing to her husband about her vision. It was probably just a foolish worry. And if something *had* happened, he — and she — would soon know.

A few minutes later, Mr. Smith was on his way to join the children. He said he would return with them around eight o'clock.

Mrs. Smith knew that if Johnny was really in danger, her husband would call. So she sat by the phone, waiting nervously for it to ring. But it never did. Still feeling uneasy, but assuring herself that it had been a foolish worry after all, Mrs.

Smith left the house to go to a meeting.

Several hours later, when Mrs. Smith returned home, she was greeted by her excited husband. He told her how Johnny had drifted out to sea in his boat. No one had noticed, and no one *would* have noticed if Johnny hadn't been screaming "Mommy! Mommy!" Luckily, Johnny had stayed in the boat, shouting, until help arrived.

"When did it happen?" Mrs. Smith asked, shaking.

"Sometime around three o'clock," answered her husband. "Why?"

Was it just a coincidence that Mrs. Smith's vision of Johnny in danger occurred exactly at three o'clock? *Or was it actually a case of ESP?*

Case #2:

"He Needs Me"

Steve and Julie were brother and sister. They were part of a big family, but these two were especially close. They liked to do their farm chores together and to run in the fields afterward. Sometimes, they played games together. One of their favorites was a mind-reading game.

They liked to play the mind-reading game when they were working in different parts of the farm. If Steve's job was to care for the horses in the barn, for example, and Julie was going to work in the fields, they would set up a special time, like two o'clock, for sending messages to each other. At the designated time, Julie would think really hard about something. She would concentrate only on that thing. Then she would imagine that the thing she was thinking about was going into Steve's head. Steve, over in the barn, would try to keep his mind blank. He would try to receive Julie's thought; and then, when he had decided that he had the thought, he would send a message back to Julie.

They got pretty good at it, they thought. And they played the game from the time they were very young until Julie left home.

Julie was in high school when her father sent her to Iowa for the summer to help out her married sister. The hardest part of leaving the farm was leaving Steve. But the two promised that if they needed each other, they would get in touch.

Julie really liked living in Iowa. She decided to stay and go to school there. She got a job helping out a woman in exchange for room and board. Julie liked the woman and she loved the independence of supporting herself and living on her own.

Julie had been in Iowa for two years when one night, around 11:45, she woke up terribly frightened. She was sure that Steve needed her! She quickly dressed and packed her suitcase.

The woman she lived with heard Julie moving

around and came to see if something was wrong. "Are you all right?" she asked.

"I've got to go home," said Julie. "My brother needs me."

"Don't be silly," said the woman. "How could you possibly know that? I'm sure you've had a bad dream. No one has come by to give us a message. Go back to sleep."

But Julie knew her feeling was more than a bad dream. Something was really wrong. Steve needed her. She had to see him. The woman insisted that Julie should at least check before dashing off. Since they had no phone, the woman suggested that they send a telegram in the morning.

Julie was determined to get home to Steve, but since neither one of the women knew when the night train came through town, Julie decided she would wait until morning. Then she would take the earliest train she could get.

Julie and the woman were eating an early breakfast the next morning, when there was a knock on the door.

"Telegram for you, miss," said the delivery man. Julie opened the telegram with trembling fingers, knowing it was about Steve. It was.

Steve had been badly hurt when his horse had

fallen on him. *And the accident had occurred at 11:30 the night before, just about fifteen minutes before Julie had awakened with the knowledge that Steve needed her!*

Case #3:

The White Room

The following story is told in the words of a young lady who lived in England in the 1800's. It was recorded in Phantasms of the Living, a book about strange happenings that was first published in 1886.

I was walking in a country lane near the place where my parents resided. I was reading geometry as I walked along, a subject little likely to produce fancies or morbid phenomena of any kind, when, in a moment, I saw a bedroom known as the White Room in my home, and upon the floor lay my mother, to all appearances dead. The vision must have remained some minutes, during which time my real surroundings appeared to pale and die out; but as the vision faded, my actual surroundings came back, at first dimly, and then clearly.

I could not doubt that what I had seen was real, so, instead of going home, I went at once to the house of our medical man and found him at home. He at once set out with me for my home, on the way putting questions I could not answer, as my mother was to all appearances well when I left home.

I led the doctor straight to the White Room, where we found my mother actually lying as in my vision. This was true even to minute details. She had been seized suddenly by an attack at the heart, and would soon have breathed her last but for the doctor's arrival.

Case #4:

An Adventure at Sea

Another story retold from Phantasms of the Living.

Life at sea wasn't easy for thirteen-year-old Adam. Because he was the youngest crew member on board ship, he was always getting bossed around. And Adam was often given the worst jobs to do.

One evening, the ship was moored just off the South Sea island of Bali. The sea was especially rough. A giant wave had capsized one of the smaller boats and washed it up on shore. Adam and some of the other crew members were about to go after it, when the ship's mate decided that they should wait until dawn.

They set out the next morning in a heavy sea. The pounding waves were huge, and the rescue boat bounced from side to side. Suddenly, Adam felt himself fly out of the boat into the ocean. He was swept underwater by the waves, then tossed into the air and swept under again. While he was under, he saw his family, all sitting in their living room. He saw his mother and sisters. He saw their faces clearly and he saw the furniture and the venetian blinds. Then he surfaced again. "Mother! Mother!" he screamed.

The other crew members heard his cries and pulled him to safety. But once the danger was over, they teased him. "Boy, what were you calling for your mother for? Do you think she could pull you out of Davy Jones's locker?" Adam was humiliated. It was bad enough being thirteen. Now he had to live with this.

Months later, Adam returned to his family in England. His near drowning was still a vivid memory. While he was telling his mother the story, she stopped him. "Why, yes," she said. "I heard you cry for me."

Adam's sister told the story this way: "I distinctly remember the incident...it made such an impression on my mind, I shall never forget it.

We were sitting quietly at work one evening; it was about nine o'clock. I think it must have been late in the summer as we had left the street door open. We first heard a faint cry of 'Mother'; we all looked up, and said to one another, 'Did you hear that? Someone cried out "Mother." ' We had scarcely finished speaking, when the voice again called, 'Mother,' twice in succession, the last cry a frightened, agonizing cry. We all started up, and Mother said to me, 'Go to the door and see what is the matter.' I ran directly into the street and stood for some minutes, but all was silent and not a person to be seen; it was a lovely evening, not a breath of air. Mother was sadly upset about it. I remember she paced the room and feared that something had happened to Adam. She wrote down the date the next day, and when Adam came home and told us how nearly he had been drowned, and the time of day, Father said it would be about the time nine o'clock would be with us. I know the date and the time corresponded."

Case #5:   .

"Guess What, Daddy"

Dr. Johnson was a doctor in a small town. He was a conscientious doctor who, after his office hours every day, made house calls to the bedridden.

One evening Dr. Johnson was just leaving the home of one of his patients. He was going down some stairs when, suddenly, a picture flashed through his head. He saw his four-year-old daughter lying at the foot of the stairs at his home.

The picture in his mind was extremely vivid. He could see her face and even the clothes she was wearing. He could also see that her chin was bleeding. Dr. Johnson looked at his watch. It was 5:35.

Dr. Johnson was alarmed, but knowing that his daughter was not home alone, and fairly sure she had not been seriously hurt, he finished visiting his patients. Several hours later, when the doctor walked in the house, he was greeted by his daughter. Her chin was bandaged. "Guess what, Daddy," she said. "I fell down the stairs!"

Dr. Johnson asked his wife when the accident had taken place. *It had happened at exactly 5:35!*

Dreams and E S P

Some scientists think that our extra-sensory perception is especially strong while we are sleeping. When we are asleep, our other senses are resting, and we cannot fight back any ESP messages by telling ourselves they are impossible.

There is a great deal of research going on in which scientists are trying to analyze the connection between ESP and dreams.

Throughout history, people have told stories of strange dreams that give information to the dreamer about an event *before* it happens — dreams that actually predict the future.

Case #1:

A Dream of Disaster

Dr. Peterson was moaning in his sleep. He was having a dream in which he saw the back part of a train sticking out of a tunnel. Suddenly, another train rammed into the first one, and the cars crumpled. They piled on top of one another, then rolled off the tracks. Dr. Peterson could hear the cries of wounded passengers. Clouds of steam hissed out of the wreckage.

Alarmed by his strange noises, Mrs. Peterson quickly woke her husband. He told her about his dream. Once he was reassured that it was "only a dream," he settled back into sleep.

Four hours later, Dr. Peterson was having breakfast. He was listening to the radio when an

emergency bulletin broke into the scheduled program. Two trains had just collided about 75 miles from Dr. Peterson's house. One of them had nearly passed through the tunnel when it was hit by the other. Steam was hissing from the engine, and the many injured passengers were being rushed to the hospital.

Perhaps it is not unusual for doctors to have dreams about emergencies. But in this dream, Dr. Peterson saw the details of the accident *exactly as they happened!*

Case #2:

The Dream Was So Real

There had been many car thefts in Cleveland, Ohio, that year. Cars were disappearing constantly. Apparently, they were being stolen and immediately driven out of the state.

When Mrs. Davis went to church one Sunday morning, she parked her car in the church parking lot. Later, when she came out of church, the car was gone. Mrs. Davis quickly called the police. They took all the information about the missing car, and filed a report. Then they turned to Mrs. Davis. "M'am," they told her, "we hate to tell you this, but you'll probably never see that car again."

Mrs. Davis's daughter was very upset about the

missing car. She couldn't get it out of her mind. Then, two nights after the car was stolen, she dreamed about it. In her dream, she saw the car parked on a particular street about fifteen miles from where she lived.

The next morning, Mrs. Davis's daughter told her husband about the dream. "It was so real," she said. "I'm going to drive over and have a look."

When she arrived at the street that had appeared in her dream, the car was sitting there. She couldn't believe it! She spoke to some people who were standing around. They told her that the car had been left there *only five minutes before she arrived!*

Case #3:

The Strange Dream of
Abraham Lincoln

President Abraham Lincoln had a dream that haunted him. He told it to his wife, and he also told it to a friend, Ward H. Lamon. Lamon later included Lincoln's account of the dream in his book, Life of Abraham Lincoln, which was published in 1872. The following story is in Lincoln's own words:

About ten days ago, I retired very late...I could not have been long in bed when I fell into a slumber, for I was weary. I soon began to dream.

There seemed to be a deathlike stillness about me. Then I suddenly heard subdued sobs, as if a number of people were weeping. I thought I left my bed and wandered downstairs. There the silence was broken by the same pitiful sobbing, but the mourners were invisible. I went from room to room; no living person was in sight, but the same mournful sounds of distress met me as I passed along.

It was light in all the rooms; every object was familiar to me, but where were all the people who were grieving as if their hearts would break? I was puzzled and alarmed.

What could be the meaning of all this? Determined to find the cause of things so mysterious and so shocking, I kept on until I arrived at the East Room, which I entered. There was a sickening surprise. Before me was a catafalque on which rested a corpse wrapped in funeral vestments. Around it were stationed soldiers who were acting as guards; and there was a throng of people, some were gazing mournfully upon the corpse whose face was covered; others were weeping pitifully.

President Abraham Lincoln (shown here with his youngest son Tad) had a terrifying dream of death that actually came true.

"Who is dead in the White House?" I demanded of one of the soldiers.

"The President," was his answer. "He was killed by an assassin."

There came a loud burst of grief from the crowd, which awoke me from my dream. I slept no more that night, and although it was only a dream, I have been strangely annoyed by it ever since.

Seventeen days later Abraham Lincoln was dead — from an assassin's bullet.

3

Backward Knowing

One kind of ESP involves knowing about people, events, or places from the past. People who claim to have this sort of experience feel almost as if they are "going back in time."

One explanation for this kind of ESP is that people may be remembering information that has been stored in their brains from the time they were very young.

But not every story can be explained so simply . . . .

Had They Been There Before?

Mr. and Mrs. Bralorne had never been out of the United States before. Now they were on a world cruise and loving every minute of it. They were enjoying the company of the other passengers and the tours of new, exotic places. They were especially excited when the ship docked in India, a country they knew little about but were eager to visit.

As the couple walked through the streets of Bombay, Mr. Bralorne had a strange feeling. Somehow, he sensed that he had been there before. But, of course, that was ridiculous. Yet, why did he know where he was?

"When we round that corner," he said to his wife, "we'll come to the Afghan Church." And when they turned the corner, the church was there.

A little while later, he remarked, "Two streets down and we'll find DeLisle Road." It was there.

Mrs. Bralorne gave him a strange look. She too was experiencing an eerie feeling that she was seeing familiar things.

That evening, back on board ship, the Bralornes discussed the situation. Both seemed to remember a certain house at the foot of Malabar Hill. They remembered a giant banyan tree in the front yard. To test themselves, they decided to see if the house was really there.

When they visited the spot the next day, there was no trace of the house or the tree. They were both relieved. Mrs. Bralorne was convinced they both had imagined the whole thing. Mr. Bralorne, however, felt uneasy. He couldn't explain the strong feeling he had about the house and the tree. He could almost see them on that spot. Turning to a nearby policeman, he inquired if a large, private house had ever stood on that site.

The answer was immediate. "One of the

greatest houses of the city once stood there, sir,"
answered the policeman. "It was torn down
about ninety years ago, but I heard about it from
my father."

Mrs. Bralorne asked nervously, "Would you
know if a giant banyan tree was in the front
yard?"

The policeman nodded. "I heard about that

too, for it was a very large one. The family who lived in the house was the Bhan family."

Mrs. Bralorne trembled; Mr. Bralorne turned pale. Both hurried back to the ship. A friend reassured them. "You probably read more about Bombay than you remember."

"Perhaps," Mr. Bralorne said. "But when our son was born, we gave him an unusual name. At the time it seemed most fitting, and we both assumed we'd seen it in some book or other. Our son was baptized Bhan Bralorne!"

Had the Bralornes read about Bombay or seen a film on India—and forgotten? That could be one explanation. But their experience seemed to go beyond just mere coincidence—especially since the Bralornes even named their son after the family they, somehow, knew so much about.

A Ghostly Kind of E S P

Glasses fall off shelves…bottles pop their tops …dishes whirl themselves across the kitchen — and no one is seen doing any of these things!

When a number of objects seem to move around by themselves, some people think a poltergeist (pol'-ter-geist) may be the cause. *Poltergeist* is a German word meaning "noisy ghost."

One theory about poltergeists is that they always seem to occur around a particular person, usually a teenager who is angry and upset. The person's problems may make his or her ESP especially strong, somehow creating an unknown kind of energy force. Some ESP scientists think that this force may be so intense that it can actually cause objects to move.

But this theory hasn't been proven, and most poltergeist cases remain unsolved mysteries. The following stories are two of the strangest and most baffling cases on record.

Weird Crashes In A Warehouse:

The Case of the
Miami Poltergeist

Every year, tourists flock to Miami Beach, Florida, from all over the country. They come to this famous vacation spot to swim, sunbathe, or just walk along the beach. They stay for a week, a month, sometimes for several months. Then, before they leave, they fill their suitcases with souvenirs for the folks back home.

Souvenirs are a big business in Miami, and many people make a good living selling them. George was the part-owner of a big souvenir company. The inside of his warehouse was filled with row upon row of shelves packed with souvenirs for tourists: glasses painted with pink flamingos, coffee mugs labeled "Miami," address books with lizard covers, shell-decorated boxes, toy alligators.

George knew his stock; he knew what was selling and what wasn't. He also knew how much was breaking. And it was way too much.

Too many things were falling off the shelves. It cost George money when things broke, so he decided to have a little talk with his workers.

"Move things back from the edge," he told his staff. "Round things have to be placed on the shelves so that they can't roll off. Look!" George picked up a coffee mug. "If you put these mugs like this, tops down, there's no way they can be jarred off."

With these instructions, George started to walk away. But before he reached the end of the aisle, one of the mugs had crashed to the floor. *No one was near the shelf!*

While George and his employees were inspecting the broken mug, a box of backscratchers crashed to the floor on the other side of the room.

Then, for the next three days, it was as if the souvenirs had a life of their own. Glasses zinged across the room. Whole boxes of souvenirs tumbled from high shelves. While the workers were cleaning up one mess, things on the other side of the room would come crashing down.

It all sounds like a wacky movie. But it wasn't funny at all to the people who worked in George's warehouse. It was a frightening experience, and a costly one.

Everyone became extra careful. They inspected all the shelves and pushed any breakable items far from the edge. Nothing seemed to help, and after about two weeks of crashes, George called in the police.

"This guy has got to be a nut," thought the policeman assigned to the case. He listened to the stories patiently, politely, and without comment; and he took notes. But to himself he thought, "Oh, yeah, right. The box just flew across the room without help from anyone. Oh sure."

But while the policeman was taking notes, a glass crashed near him. There was no one around. Then something *else* fell. And something else. No one had touched the shelves. "Wow," thought the policeman. "They'll never believe me if I write this stuff down on a report." So he called for some more police witnesses.

Three more police officers joined him. They checked to see if the shelves were wobbly or if any objects were too close to the edge. They waited and watched. They watched every person in the room...just in case someone was staging the breakage.

A box crashed down. No one was anywhere near it.

The police officers inspected the area around the fallen box. They were looking for a string or some elastic, anything that would explain the strange occurrence. But they found nothing. Just a fallen box, filled with address books.

A few weeks after the crashes began, people became suspicious of nineteen-year-old Eddie, a stock clerk at the warehouse. His job was to keep the shelves stocked and to help get the orders together. Strangely enough, the crashes happened only when Eddie was around.

When he was out of the room, everything was calm. When he came back in, the breaking began again. But no one ever caught Eddie throwing things or setting up tricks. Some things happened close to where he was standing. Other crashes were far away from him.

Investigators from the Parapsychology Laboratory at Duke University were called in. Parapsychology is the study of events and happenings that seem to have no reasonable explanation.

The investigators felt that Eddie was somehow involved. They talked to Eddie, and gave him tests to see how he was feeling about himself. The tests showed that Eddie was angry at the world. He felt that his life was a mess, and that people were unfair to him. At home Eddie fought with his family. At night, he had terrible nightmares. It was clear that Eddie had emotional problems.

But, just the fact that Eddie had problems really didn't prove anything. A lot of people have problems — but no poltergeists show up.

Shortly after the investigators left, Eddie quit his job, and the flying objects stopped flying. Was it a coincidence — or did Eddie's emotional state create the disturbance? The mystery of the "Miami Poltergeist" was never solved.

The Case
of the Long Island Poltergeist

The case of the Long Island, New York, poltergeist began with a broken statue. When twelve-year-old Mike Taylor walked into his room after school, he discovered that a ceramic statue had been smashed. Also broken was the model ship that had been next to it on the dresser. "It's nothing," thought Mike. "Things accidentally break all the time."

Then Mrs. Taylor noticed something strange in her room. A bottle of water had fallen over; the top had somehow unscrewed, and the water had spilled. "Strange," she thought, "but nothing to get excited about. Probably carelessness."

Then the noises began—popping and spilling

noises that seemed to come from all over the house. When the Taylors checked, they found two more spilled bottles in the bathroom. The tops had come unscrewed. In the kitchen, under the sink, a bottle of starch had spilled all over the cabinet.

What happened next made the Taylors decide to take some action. Mike was in the bathroom brushing his teeth, and Mr. Taylor was standing in the doorway of the bathroom. All of a sudden two bottles which had been placed on the top of the vanity table started to move. Mr. Taylor reported that one bottle moved straight ahead. The other one, he claimed, moved around at a 45-degree angle. The first bottle rolled into the sink; the other one crashed to the floor!

That was it for the Taylors. They called the police.

When Patrolman Connors arrived, he gathered all the Taylors in the living room and began to question them. Exactly what had happened? Where were they when the poppings and spillings occurred?

The Taylors were telling their story when all of a sudden, they heard noises in the bathroom. All, including the patrolman, went to investigate. They found that a bottle of medicine had spilled again! It was lying on its side. The Taylors had cleaned up the mess from the last time, and Patrolman Connors had just inspected the bathroom. There had been no bottles lying on their sides. "I can swear to that," said Connors.

Altogether, there were 67 instances of spilled or flying objects in the Taylor house. Bottles, statues, globes, pictures, lamps, and bowls flew through the house. Even bookcases were mysteriously overturned!

The strange occurrences soon became a news item. Papers across the country were telling the story of the "Long Island Poltergeist."

The news reached Dr. J. B. Rhine in North Carolina. Dr. Rhine was head of the Parapsychology Laboratory at Duke University. When Dr. Rhine read about the Taylor case, he contacted them. He also called the police who were doing the investigation. Then he sent his staff to the scene.

Dr. Rhine's people arrived at the Taylor house determined to conduct a scientific investigation. If there was a natural cause of the bottle poppings and flying objects, they would find it. They had had experience in this kind of thing and knew what to look for.

Dr. J.B. Rhine, who was head of the Parapsychology Laboratory at Duke University. It was Dr. Rhine who first used the term "extra-sensory perception" (ESP) to describe certain kinds of strange happenings.

The first step was to talk to the Taylors. Dr. Pratt and Dr. Roll, the investigators, wanted to hear every detail of every incident. They especially wanted to know the exact location of each family member when all the weird things were happening. An overturned bottle, they knew, might have been turned over by somebody's hand; a statue might have been yanked across the room with a string by a person on the other end.

The investigators listened carefully, took notes, and made charts. They also examined the police records. Most of the incidents had been reported by the Taylors to the police, and there were detailed reports in the police files.

The investigators also talked to each family member separately. They wanted to find out if the Taylors were a respectable family. Perhaps they were all making up the stories. Perhaps they had gotten together and dreamed up the poltergeist.

But after all the talks were over, the reports studied, and all the incidents carefully explored, the investigators became convinced that the Taylors were responsible, honest people. They were not the sort of family to create a hoax.

But suppose one member of the family had managed to fool all the others? The attention focused on Mike. Mike had been around for all the incidents, and he had been the first one to discover the broken statue. It became clear that Mike could have opened bottles before they were discovered, and he could have spilled things when no one was looking. He might also have created the noises long after he had done the spilling. Then he could be far away from the scene of the spilled liquids when they were discovered later. Was it all just a boyish prank?

There were many incidents that Mike could have caused. At one time, the police and even Mike's father thought he was the culprit. But there were many that Mike could not have caused. When all the facts were in, the investigators decided that the occurrences could probably not be attributed to Mike. There were too many incidents that couldn't be traced to him.

Perhaps, they thought, some outside vibrations were causing the objects to move. Doctors Pratt and Roll checked for high-frequency waves. They checked for underground springs, gas leaks, bad wiring, faulty electrical connections. They found nothing.

Roll and Pratt were particularly baffled by the way the bottles seemed to unscrew their tops. There had been 23 incidents with bottles. In nearly all of them, the tops had come off. Had someone figured out a chemical way to make it happen?

The investigators experimented with "dry ice." Dry ice is the solid state of carbon dioxide. As it sits in a warm temperature, a solid hunk of dry ice turns back into the gas, carbon dioxide. If the dry ice is out in the open, the gas disappears into the air. But suppose someone drops dry ice into a bottle and screws the bottle top back on. Since the gas has nowhere to go, it will build up pressure inside the bottle. The pressure inside the bottle from the carbon dioxide gas might build up so much that the top would loosen and come unscrewed.

Hopeful that they had at last solved the mystery, the investigators experimented by dropping hunks of dry ice into some bottles. Then, they screwed the tops back on and waited for the pressure to build up. But the pressure never did build up enough to unscrew the bottles. Instead, the gas just seeped through the closed top.

Next, the investigators tried tightening the tops mechanically. They hoped that the supertight tops would leave no room for the gas to escape. The pressure built up. But then, when the pressure became too great for the bottle, the top didn't unscrew at all. The whole neck of the bottle burst! The dry ice experiments had led to a dead end.

After ten days with the Taylors, the investigators returned to their laboratory at Duke with no answers. They had found no natural causes for the strange occurrences and no reason to suspect a prankster. All they had found was the universal poltergeist ingredient — a young person, Mike, around whom the strange occurrences seemed to have revolved.

Could Mike, without knowing it, have sent out some unknown kind of energy that had caused all those objects to move? No one has been able to answer that question.

Is It Magic—Or E S P?

The stories that follow are about two men who claim to have special powers of ESP. Uri Geller claims that he has the ability to move objects with his mind. Peter Hurkos says he can find out all about a person by holding one of his or her belongings in his hands.

There are many people, including scientists, who have witnessed Uri Geller and Peter Hurkos up close. Some have declared that both men are terrific magicians, nothing more. But some are convinced that the two men do have special powers.

Uri Geller

When Uri Geller was three or four years old, his favorite place to play was a garden across from his house in Tel Aviv, Israel. It was a lush, quiet garden, with a pond and huge shade trees.

One afternoon, Uri was playing there when, in his words, "Suddenly there was a very loud, high-pitched ringing in my ears. All other sounds stopped. Something made me look up at the sky.... There was a silvery mass of light.... I felt as if I had been knocked over backward. There was a sharp pain in my forehead. Then I was knocked out."*

Uri Geller still remembers that moment clearly.

*Geller, Uri, *My Story*, Praeger, New York, New York, 1975.

He feels that something happened to him that day; something that perhaps explains why he has always been "different" from other people.

Uri says that he first realized this difference when he was about six years old. His father had given him a watch. Uri liked to sit in his class at school and look at the watch from time to time, waiting for class to be over. One day, after Uri had looked away for a while, he noticed that his watch was half an hour fast. He set it back to the correct time.

Over the next few weeks, Uri discovered that his watch kept jumping ahead half an hour. He had to keep setting it back. When it started to jump four and five hours, Uri decided that the watch was no good. He left it home.

At home, without Uri, the watch ran perfectly. So he put it on again. This time Uri stared at it all day. He wanted to catch the watch moving. He did. Suddenly, the hands on his watch went crazy. They kept spinning around the dial. Uri gave up on the watch.

Months later, his parents got him a new watch. He proudly wore it to school. Then, in the middle of the day, the hands on the new watch began to curl. When they bumped into the crystal, they bent sideways. By the time Uri got home, the new watch was ruined. Uri claims that he had never opened the watch. The hands had just bent by themselves.

Soon after that, another strange thing happened. Uri was eating some soup, when suddenly the spoon bent. Soup spilled all over his lap.

During the next months, things like this happened over and over again. Objects would bend while Uri held them. Then it happened to spoons and forks that he wasn't even holding. Spoons lying on the table out of his reach would bend all by themselves.

As Uri grew older, he discovered more and more things about himself. He found that he could receive messages from other people's minds. One day his teacher gave the class an assignment to write a story. When the class handed the papers in, the teacher discovered that Uri had written the same paper, practically word for word, as a boy who was sitting five seats behind Uri. Neither boy had left his seat.

After a while, Uri learned to use his special talents. He could guess what numbers people were thinking. He could draw the same pictures that a friend was drawing, even when the friend was far away. People began to ask him questions

Uri Geller claims that he can bend objects by just
concentrating on them. Here he poses with silverware
that is definitely out of shape!

about his strange talent. They asked him to perform for classes and assemblies.

By the time Uri was an adult, he began giving demonstrations of his "power" all over Israel. He would ask members of the audience to write or draw things on a blackboard. Then he would "receive" their messages, and tell them what they had written. He would ask them to bring in their broken watches. Uri had discovered that he could fix watches with his mind, without even touching them.

And he would bend things. It was the bending that made Uri famous all over the world. People would hold keys in their hands. Uri would gently stroke the key with his finger. Suddenly, the key would bend. He also did it with spoons and pieces of metal.

Some of the strangest stories about Uri happened when he was appearing on radio and TV. He would tell the people listening to concentrate on trying to bend something in their own homes. Sometimes he suggested that if they had a broken watch, they should concentrate on trying to make it run. Then, together with his whole listening audience, Uri would concentrate.

Nearly every time Uri asked his listening audience to participate in his experiments, hundreds of people would call up the station to report that it had worked. Spoons had bent. Watches that hadn't run for months would start again. One lady in Germany even reported that dozens of kitchen utensils and silverware in her house had bent in their drawers!

As news about Uri's strange powers spread, many scientists became intrigued. They wanted to test him in a laboratory setting to see if he was just a terrific magician, or if he really did have some strange power that would shake up the scientific world.

Uri was examined and tested by scientists in England, Germany, and the United States. They searched him before they performed their tests. They made careful plans so that no one could possibly know the answer or be able to help him in any way.

In one case, scientists at the Stanford Research Center in California, tested Uri to see whether he could really influence objects he wasn't touching. In a room, they set up a very sensitive laboratory scale that recorded even the tiniest weight change.

To see how the scale would react, the scientists jumped up and down. They pounded on the table. They banged things together in the air.

Then, the scientists placed a small weight on the scale and put a glass jar over the scale so that air current wouldn't affect the weight.

Uri was searched and then brought into the room. He stood near the scale without moving and held his hands several inches above the jar. He made faces. He ground his teeth. He frowned.

An audience of scientists watched to see that there were no tricks. They saw the scale register changes. At one point, the scale registered 100 times the weight that the scientists had been able to register with their banging, jumping, and pounding. Uri had changed the weight without touching the scale. Could he really have done it with his mind?

Many scientists have been baffled by the feats of Uri Geller. But many magicians say that Uri is such a fantastic magician that he can even fool the scientists. Is it magic—or an especially powerful kind of ESP? It's hard to tell.

Peter Hurkos

There's a certain amount of risk in painting a house—especially when you're balancing yourself on a high ladder. But Peter Hurkos was used to taking risks. He had been a sailor. He had been a spy against the Germans during World War II. And he had been helping his father in the painting business ever since he was a little boy.

So, on that day in 1941, Peter Hurkos wasn't bothered a bit as he climbed the ladder, paint and paint brush in hand. But accidents happen even to the confident. Peter lost his balance and he fell 35 feet to the ground. He landed on his head.

"I think if I hadn't partially landed on my shoulder," he said later, "I would have died."

Peter was seriously injured. He had a bad concussion, and the doctors weren't sure whether he would live. For three days, Peter was unconscious in the hospital. Then, on the fourth day, Peter regained his consciousness. His family, his friends, and his doctors were delighted. But Peter was troubled — he felt that something had changed inside his head.

At first, he told no one about it. Maybe, he thought, it will go away as I get better. The "it" was something very strange. As Peter lay in his hospital bed, he discovered that he knew all sorts of information about the doctors and nurses. He knew about their home lives; he knew about their problems; he knew about their activities. Yet, he had never seen them before he came to the hospital.

Peter was confused. When he told the doctors what was happening, they didn't believe him at first. They figured it was part of his injury. After all, he *had* fallen on his head. Perhaps the accident had temporarily affected his sanity.

Peter began to tell them facts about themselves, facts that had just come into his head from nowhere. The doctors were stunned. There was no way Peter could have known those facts. The doctors had never mentioned anything about themselves in his presence. Not even when he was unconscious!

The doctors tried to figure out what had changed inside Peter's head. They took X-rays. They gave him medical and psychological tests. But the tests showed nothing — nothing that could explain Peter's weird talent.

Peter claims that it was difficult for him to get used to his new talent. When he was in a room full of people, he would be bombarded with information about the people present. Sometimes he would tell the people what he knew about them. People would suddenly discover that he knew their secrets. This total stranger knew things about them that they didn't want anyone to know! People would be embarrassed and hurt. They would walk the other way when they saw Peter coming.

Peter learned to keep his information to himself. He also learned how to use his talent to make a living. He would appear before audiences. He would ask people in the audience to put something in an envelope — a key, a handkerchief, a letter, some clothes. Then Peter would have his helper seal the envelope and hand it to him. Peter would hold the envelope, concentrate, and tell the audience about the person who owned the object.

Peter Hurkos became well-known throughout the world. One day the police in his town in Holland called him. A child was missing and the police asked Peter to help them find her. They brought him some clothing that belonged to the child. Peter held the clothing in his hands. Sud-

(Wide World Photos)

Peter Hurkos has helped police departments find missing persons. Peter claims he can know where someone is by holding on to one of his or her belongings. Here he helps police in Falls Church, Virginia, track down a criminal.

denly, inside his head, he had a picture of the child. He also had a picture of the place where she could be found. He told the police. They followed Peter's directions and found the child.

Soon, police departments all over the world were calling Peter and asking him to help them find missing persons. Near Palm Springs, California, a plane had gone down. No one knew where. Peter asked for some clothing of the pilot and a map. He held the clothing in his hands and concentrated on the missing pilot. Then he pointed to a place on the map. The search parties were combing a vast area of 600 miles. The place Peter pointed out on the map turned out to be only one mile from the wreckage.

In another case, Peter was called by a Massachusetts official to help the Boston police department solve a crime. The police were very skeptical. What kind of quack had been called in to help them? Peter had to prove himself. He turned to one of the police investigators. "Your mother is very sick," said Peter. He described the mother's illness. The investigator turned pale. Peter had described the illness exactly.

Then Peter turned to another investigator. "Call your house," said Peter. "There is an emergency. Your daughter has something wrong with her throat." The man called home. His daughter had swallowed a safety pin! The police were convinced. They cooperated. But Peter never did solve the crime. (He presented a number of ideas to the police and even led them to one possible suspect. But the police never did gather enough actual evidence to arrest the suspect.)

Peter claims that he *has* solved many crimes. The police department in Miami, Florida, gave him an honorary badge for helping them. Other police departments have given him awards. But there are many people who claim that he led them in the wrong direction and wasted their time. In some cases, people have been arrested on Peter's advice and released later. Many police departments have been embarrassed because they have listened to him too closely. There is a lot of controversy about Peter's powers.

Peter was once asked to describe what he saw in his head. "I see pictures," he said. "Like on TV. I cannot help them. They come and go in my brain."

"What about you?" asked the interviewer. "Do you get pictures about yourself?"

"No," said Peter. "Sometimes I can't even find

my own shoes! I can find missing people, but I can't find my shoes.''

No one else has ever seen Peter's pictures. Only Peter. And, although some people claim that Peter has told them incredible things, others are highly skeptical.

Animal E S P

Some senses, like smelling and hearing, are much sharper and more sensitive in animals than in human beings. A dog whistle is silent to human ears. But dogs can hear it. Humans can neither see nor smell the path where another human being has walked. Yet bloodhounds have tracked missing people through miles of woods.

Some animals also seem to know things that go beyond the five senses. Birds have an uncanny ability. Many birds fly south for the winter. Sometimes young birds — who have never been south before—lead the way. Somehow, they just know where to go.

How do they know where to go? What kind of messages do animals receive? Perhaps if scientists discover the secrets of animal behavior, they will better understand ESP in humans.

Case #1:

Watch the Animals

On February 4, 1975, a town in China was totally destroyed by an earthquake. Over one million people lived in and around the town. Yet hardly anyone was hurt.

The townspeople had predicted that the earthquake was coming. They had saved their own lives. And they didn't do it with elaborate scientific equipment — they did it by watching their animals.

Months earlier, the government of China had noticed a strange phenomenon. Each time there was an earthquake, people reported afterward that their animals had behaved in weird ways — weeks and sometimes months — before the quake. Dogs howled. Cattle refused to graze. Horses neighed and kicked. Chickens and pigeons refused to go into their coops.

The Chinese government sent out a notice to farmers all over the country. The notice told farmers to watch their animals and to report any unusual behavior. The Chinese government called the program "The People's War against earthquakes."

A month before the February earthquake, hundreds of reports started to come in to the government from one town in particular. Perhaps the strangest report was that snakes had crawled out of their hibernation holes. Many snakes were found frozen on the top of the snow.

When the reports began to accumulate, the government warned the townspeople that an earthquake was coming. Thousands of lives were saved.

Animals and earthquakes have been studied in this country too. In one study, scientists in California noticed that a group of seventeen chimpanzees in a university laboratory had suddenly become restless. Instead of hopping and swinging around on their playground equipment as usual, the chimpanzees were spending their time on the ground. Soon after the scientists made their report, an earthquake occurred.

In 1964, there was a serious earthquake in Alaska. Just before the quake, bears came out of hibernation early and rushed into the hills.

There are many studies going on to try to determine what makes animals act so strangely just before an earthquake. What is it the animals sense, that people and their machines do not?

One theory is that animals may be supersensitive to the many changes that occur in the earth before and during an earthquake. Sound waves are altered; air pressure, electrical currents, and magnetic fields change. Even the tilt of the earth is affected. It is hard to know which changes, or combination of changes, the animals are able to "read."

In the future, as we watch our animals use their special kind of ESP, we may be able to predict not only earthquakes, but other natural disasters as well.

Strange Crying

It was the middle of the afternoon when Mrs. Hughes noticed that the dog was missing. Then she heard a whining sound coming from a crawl-space under the house. Mrs. Hughes went to check. The dog was there. He was crying in a way that Mrs. Hughes had never heard before.

Her first thought was that the dog had hurt himself in some way. She tried to get him to come out so she could comfort him or, if necessary, take him to the vet. The dog wouldn't come out. He just stayed curled up under the house whining and crying in a strange, eerie way.

When the rest of the family came home, they all tried to get the dog out from under the house. He wouldn't come.

Later in the day, the Hughes family received some tragic news. The older son had been on his way home from college when there had been a terrible automobile accident. The boy had been killed.

The time of the accident coincided exactly with the beginning of the dog's strange behavior.

Case #3:

A Long Journey

The Gregory family was moving from Aurora, Illinois, to Lansing, Michigan. Their new home was more than 200 miles from the old one. The family was looking forward to the move—except for one thing. There was no room in the new house for their dog, Tony. Before they left, the Gregorys had to give Tony away.

Six weeks after the move, Mr. Gregory was walking in downtown Lansing. A dog came leaping toward him. Mr. Gregory stared in disbelief. The dog looked like Tony! But there was no way Tony could have known where the family had moved. Tony had never been to the new house. He had never been anywhere near Lansing.

Mr. Gregory examined the dog. There was no doubt about the dog's identity. Tony was still wearing the collar Mr. Gregory had bought for him.

The Gregory family made room for Tony in their new house.

E S P and Plants

A plant is a plant. It has roots, a stem, and leaves. If you keep it watered and it receives the right light, it will grow.

There are a few other things you can do for plants: give them a little plant food now and then; give them bigger pots; wash the dust off their leaves....

But in the end, a plant is just a plant. It can't carry on a conversation, and it never tells a good joke. Mostly, it just sits there and grows. It's a decoration — pretty to look at but not very interesting to play with.

If that's what you think, the following pages may make you change your mind.

They Got the Message

Mr. Porter was about to perform an experiment. He wanted to see if plants would respond to human thoughts. He was going to plant corn kernels on two sides of a pie pan. Then he was going to be tender and kind and encouraging to the kernels on one side. He would talk to them, tell them he loved them, send them lots of "good" messages.

The corn kernels on the other half of the pan would not be so lucky. Mr. Porter was going to send them "bad" messages. He was going to let them know that he didn't want them to grow, that they didn't deserve to become corn plants.

Mr. Porter wanted to see if the seeds would respond. Was it possible, by sending good and bad messages, to make them do what he wanted them to do?

Mr. Porter worked hard to create a fair experiment. First he got a big bowl and mixed the dirt in it. Then he added water and mixed it up again.

Next, Mr. Porter got a round, ten-inch pie pan and pressed the wet dirt into it. Then, he divided the pie pan in half with a thin board. Now he was ready to plant the seeds.

Mr. Porter put all the corn kernels in a brown paper bag. He put the bag on the shelf above his eye level so that he could not see which seeds he was picking. He reached into the bag, took out the first kernel he touched, and planted it. Then he reached in again and took out another kernel. He planted the second one on the other side of the board. Altogether, Mr. Porter planted 23 kernels, one at a time, first on one side of the board, then on the other side. He tried to match the sides and keep the kernels evenly spaced.

Now it was time to choose the "good" side and the "bad" side. He gently twirled the pan around and pointed to one side. That would be the good side, the one he wanted to grow. He marked it.

Next, Mr. Porter wrapped the pie plate with a waxed paper that he couldn't see through. He sealed the paper on the bottom and set the pan down. Earlier, he had been careful to choose a dividing board that was high enough to allow the seeds to sprout.

Then it was time to start sending messages to the corn kernels. Mr. Porter had marked which side was to receive the positive messages and which side was to receive the negative messages, but he couldn't see what was happening inside the waxed paper.

For eight days Mr. Porter sent his positive and negative messages. Several times a day, for at least fifteen minutes in all, Mr. Porter concentrated on his pie plate. "Grow," he told the good side. "I want you to become strong, healthy little corn plants." He scolded the other side. "Don't grow at all."

After eight days, Mr. Porter unwrapped his pie plate. On the "good" side were sixteen tiny corn plants. On the "bad" side was one.

It's hard to believe that those corn kernels could have received Mr. Porter's messages. But that's one experiment you don't have to believe on faith. Try it yourself. Set up a similar pie pan. Treat everything equally. Make sure you use the same soil for both sides of the pan. Also make sure that the soil is uniformly wet. Pick the seeds without looking. Let a friend, who hasn't watched you plant the seeds, choose which side should receive the positive messages and which the negative. See if your experiment gets the same dramatic results.

You also might want to devise your own experiments for testing whether positive and negative messages really do affect the growth of seeds. Try planting in separate pie pans. Or try planting in one pan that receives no messages at all. Remember: You always need more than one group of seeds so that you can compare the results.

Your Plant is Listening

Jennifer Mitchell had always loved music. She went to college expecting to spend all her time studying music. She was dismayed to learn that her college required her to take a biology course to graduate.

Jennifer wasn't very interested in biology—the study of plants and animals. "Oh well," she thought, "maybe I can mix in some music with biology studies." She came up with an original idea. Jennifer had read about how plants reacted to positive messages. Suppose she did her own report about how plants reacted to music? It might be interesting.

Jennifer started her experiment simply. First, she made a tape recording of two notes on the piano—B and D. She set up her tape recorder and sat down at the piano. She taped five minutes of the notes and left five minutes of silence; then she taped another five minutes of the notes and another five minutes of silence. Jennifer filled the whole tape with notes and then silence.

Next, Jennifer collected two groups of plants. Each group had five kinds of plants: philodendrons, corn, radishes, geraniums, and African violets. The groups were placed in separate rooms. One group "listened" to the tape for twelve hours a day on a special self-winding recorder; the other group was left with silence. Both groups received the same amount of light and water.

Jennifer watched closely. For ten days nothing significant happened. But after two weeks, there was a marked change in the plants exposed to the music. The geranium leaves turned yellow and died. By the end of the third week, Jennifer reported that the corn, radishes, and philodendrons in the music room had all died. Only the African violets grew well.

The other group of plants, those in the quiet room, were fine—green and healthy. Since both groups had received the same care, it seemed possible that the music had somehow killed the plants in the first group.

People in the biology department at Jennifer's college were intrigued with her findings. They allowed her to use special rooms for her next experiment. The special rooms were called control chambers. Jennifer could be certain that in these rooms she could control the temperature, the humidity, the light, the air, the soil. All the plants would have exactly the same environment. Only the sound would be different.

In her next experiment, which lasted about two weeks, Jennifer used three groups of plants. One group "listened" to a tape recording of the note F, constantly for eight hours each day. The second group "listened" to the F for a total of three hours a day. And the third group had silence.

Jennifer reported that all the plants in the eight-hour-a-day room were dead within two weeks. The plants in the three-hour room were thriving. In fact, the three-hour plants were even healthier than the plants that had had no sound at all!

By the next year, the whole biology department at Jennifer's college was mixing plants and music. One group of women experimented with squash plants. In one control chamber, the squash plants "listened" to rock and roll radio all day. In another chamber, another group of squash plants "listened" to classical music.

Squash plants have vines that crawl along the ground as they grow. The women reported that the squashes listening to classical music crawled toward the speaker that the music came from. In fact, they seemed to "like" the music so much that they began to grow around the speaker, clinging to it as they twined around!

In the rock music room, the squash plants grew *away* from the speaker, as though they were trying to escape!

One group of scientists who performed plant-music experiments reported that plants growing with constant rock music were smaller than those exposed to silence or classical music. Some of the rock-music plants developed crooked stems and weird-shaped leaves!

Other experiments have suggested that gentle music makes plants grow better. A scientist in India played the violin for his mimosa plants every morning. He reported that the plants grew twice as fast as the plants that were not serenaded.

Experimenters around the world have reported

that plants are affected by music. But scientists are not satisfied by these reports. They want to know *why*.

One scientist suggests that the openings in the plant leaves, called *stomata*, stay open longer when music is being played. The longer the stomata are open, he suggests, the more time the plant has to be stimulated.

Another scientist suggests that vibrations in the air which are caused by the music have an effect on the plant. Still another scientist thinks vibrations in the ground cause the plants to react.

No one really has the answers. Everyone's theory is just that—a theory. Until the plants can talk to us, we probably won't know. And of course, the plants will never be able to talk to us. Or will they?

A Final Word About E S P

There are many stories about extra-sensory experiences. There have even been laboratory tests in universities throughout the world that seem to lead to the conclusion that ESP does exist. But none of the universities, and none of the best scientific minds in the world have been able to tell us *what* ESP is, *why* it is, or *how* it works.

The science of parapsychology, which studies this extra-sensory world is still a baby science. There is so much about ESP that is unknown. There are so many mysteries. Many more years of research are necessary—and many serious scientists are needed to do that research.

Perhaps someone reading this book will someday become an ESP scientist, and try to solve the mystery of extra-sensory perception. The challenge is there.

GLOSSARY

Below are some terms which are often used to describe different kinds of ESP:

Clairvoyance (Clair-voy′ance)—Knowing about an object, person, event, or situation without the use of the five senses. A person may see details of a distant scene almost as if he or she were actually looking at it.

Precognition (Pre-cog-nish′-un)—To know about an event or situation *before* it happens, often by dreaming about it.

Psychokinesis (Sy-ko-ke′ne-sis) — Making objects move or change by concentrating on them. Uri Geller claims to have this power.

Psychometry (Sy-ko′me-tree)—Knowing about a person by holding on to one of his or her belongings.

Retrocognition (Retro-cog-nish′-un)—Knowing, in detail, about people, events, or places from the past without having read or been told about them.
   The word retrocognition means ''backward knowing.''

Telepathy (Tel-e′pathy) — Knowing what is going on in someone else's mind without being told.